ENDORSEMENTS

"I have known Vicky for a number of years and have been witness to her vibrant relationship with the Lord. I have found her prayers always to be timely in their delivery and an encouraging reminder of the great love God has for each and every one of us."

— *Janet Westlund, MSW, LICSW*

"I always look forward to receiving Vicky's weekly prayers. I find them to be centering, and they bring me back to what is important in my day."

— *Ann Alger, RN*

Tricia:
This book was written by my cousin. Hope you enjoy it & it brings you peace.

Love, Mom

Christmas
2015

A Little Book of Christian Prayers

FEATHER

ON THE

WATER

VICTORIA ERBELE

ISBN: 978-1-940014-49-4

Library of Congress Catalog Number: 2015930269
Printed in the United States of America
First Printing: 2015
19 18 17 16 15   5 4 3 2 1

Cover design by Nupoor Gordon
Interior design by Kris Vetter

Wise Ink Creative Publishing
222 N. 2nd Street Suite 220
Minneapolis, MN 55401
www.wiseinkpub.com

To order, visit www.itascabooks.com or call 1-800-901-3480. Reseller discounts available.

All Scripture quotations are from the New American Standard Bible. Reference Edition, Collins.

DEDICATION

I dedicate this work to my friend Lillian, who has been by my side through many difficult times through the years. Lillian is a faithful servant to God and has blessed many lives, including mine, with her faithfulness!

TABLE OF CONTENTS

INTRODUCTION

God's love for each of us is awesome! I am always amazed at God's patience as he waited for me to totally surrender to him. Allowing God into every part of my life gives me great joy. As I have learned of his great love, I have been inspired to write these prayers. For me, there is no life without God's presence!

I believe these prayers are inspired by the Holy Spirit. It was a surprise when they were coming to mind, and I was able to express them in writing. I learned so much as I analyzed and chose the verses that accompany each prayer. Many of the prayers are reflections of my experiences over the years—the years that I feel were in preparation for me to share these thoughts. It is only by God's faithfulness that this is possible! These themes are meaningful to me and my hope is that they will be to you also.

Nature has been my refuge since an early age and it inspired many of these prayers. As a child, much of my free time was spent wandering the "cedar swamp" on my parents' farm. Many lessons have been learned from observing the world God has made. He has given us so much to enjoy! Many hours of meditation while gardening, bird watching, camping, canoeing, and spending time in the woods helped me enjoy the symphony of nature God has provided. The "Feather on the Water" prayer is from an experience I had while kayaking on a peaceful, quiet lake. I felt especially close to the Lord that day, and felt in my heart that I should share it!

I believe the Bible was written to be applicable through the ages. The principles God used in the Old Testament are the same used in the New Testament and apply to our lives today. For example, Job 28:12 says, "But where can wisdom be found? And where is the place of understanding?"

Sometimes people say that the Old Testament is made up of stories of violence and sin, and that God is a revengeful God. When I studied these stories, I found that there is a common theme: the people were asked to worship only the Lord and to follow his way for their own good. When they followed him, their lives were prolific. When they did not follow God, there was hardship.

During traumatic experiences in my life, I could not put words together for prayer. Then I read written prayers such as The Lord's Prayer, found in Matthew 6:9. It was very comforting and helpful to have written prayers during those times.

"Delight yourself in the Lord, and he will give you the desires of your heart." (Psalms 37:4). What a wonderful verse! As an immature Christian, I had many worldly desires. Today, as I continue to grow and enjoy the presence of the Lord in my life, I find my desires changing. Slowly, I have been guided into a new life that is creative and productive for the Lord. There is peace in my heart knowing that God will give me all I need. When temptation strikes, I have tools to use to get back in line!

I pray that you will enjoy reading these prayers, and that they will be helpful in your prayer life. May God bless you as you read!

FEATHER ON THE WATER

"When you pass through the waters, I will be with you."

—*Isaiah 43:2*

My Lord, my God,
Why does a feather on the water
remind me of you?
It alludes peace, quiet, and surrender.
Floating,
it flows gently with the current,
along with any breeze that comes.
Not struggling to escape,
it allows itself to go where time takes it.
O let me be like the feather, Lord,
to flow with the way you have planned for me
and not struggle to escape
or change my path.
Then I will have
peace,
contentment,
and joy!
You will be my only need.
Through Jesus Christ,
Amen!

GROWING FAITH

As we grow in our faith, we come across obstacles to overcome, mountains to climb, forks in the road, and questions to ask. With these challenges, we learn to lean on the Lord for guidance in every part of our lives and become stronger in our faith. Our trust and willingness to surrender grows when we sense his unconditional love and realize that his timing is best!

God knows all! He knows everything about us—including every little thing hidden in our hearts. When we accept this and ask for help to overcome trials and temptations, we accept him in every part of our being. God desires to help us grow in our faith. He is faithful!

"Then Jacob was left alone, and a man wrestled with him until daybreak."

—*Genesis 32:24*

My Lord, my God,
have I been wrestling with you
and not with the evil one?
How confused I become when things
do not go the way I desire!
I try to change it to my way!
I wrestle one way and then another,
and still I fail!
Only when exhaustion overtakes me
will I pause to ask you, Lord, for help.
Then I realize that it was you
I was trying to change!
I will change my ways.
You are the all-knowing God
and give what is best for me.
I will quit struggling against you,
remember your words,
and come to you when I have problems, O Lord.
Through Jesus Christ,
Amen!

"He said to him the third time, 'Simon son of John, do you love Me?' Peter was grieved because He said to him the third time, 'Do you love Me?' And he said to Him, 'Lord, You know all things; You know that I love You.' Jesus said, 'Tend my sheep.'"

—John 21:17

My Lord, Jesus, fill me with your bread of life
that I may tend your sheep.
My sustenance comes from you.
I look to you for all I need.
Fill me, Lord, with your living water,
that I may give to all to drink.
This bread and water comes only from you
and is not of my own.
Keep me filled to the brim, my God,
then I can feed your sheep
with a never-ending supply from you!
Praise God forever!
Through Jesus Christ,
Amen!

"Your kingdom Come. Your will be done, on earth as it is in Heaven."

—*Matthew 6:10*

My Precious Lord,
I ask that your will be done.
Yet I always ask, *What is your will?*
I fear that I will do otherwise.
I fail to trust you.
I seem to need you to write it on paper,
so there is no doubt what your will is!
I pray, Lord, for discernment
in my daily life,
to put complete faith and trust in you.
Guide me in the path
you have planned for me.
Thank you, Jesus, for these words.
May your will be done all over the world!
Through Jesus Christ,
Amen!

"For the Lord is watching His children, listening to their prayers."

—*1 Peter 3:12*

Why should I question you, O Lord,
when your timing is not like mine?
I want my requests to be answered
in earthly time.
You have your heavenly time and plan for all things.
I become impatient;
I think I know how and when
you should answer my prayer.
But is it then really a prayer?
Or is it a demand?
Sometimes many years pass
waiting for a blessing from you.
When I receive it, it is much sweeter
than what I imagined!
When I wait, my prayers are answered
in a gentle, sweet way
that I could not have planned for myself.
Sometimes, I forget
about what I have prayed for.
Then you show me that you do not forget!
Through Jesus Christ,
Amen!

"While they were eating, Jesus took some bread, and after a blessing, He broke it and gave it to His disciples, and said, 'Take, eat; this is My body.'"

—*Matthew 26:26*

Precious Jesus,
you gave up your throne in Heaven,
and died a humiliating death for me.
Lord, how can I show my gratitude?
You gave your human life
that I may live eternally.
You came to earth
to fulfill the law
and teach me how to live.
You showed me how to commune with you
by breaking bread with others.
By doing this, I will remember
all that you have done for me!
Each day, Lord,
I will lift my hands to Heaven
and praise your name!
My wonderful Jesus,
I pray in your name,
Amen!

"Behold, I am laying in Zion a stone, a tested stone, a costly cornerstone for the foundation, firmly placed . . ."

—*Isaiah 28:16*

Lord, I came upon a stone, heavy and solid.
I could not move it.
It was an obstacle in my path.
Could there be treasure beneath it?
I could make a new path around it
or chisel it apart and continue on my way.
The stone may protect me from an enemy
or from the weather.
I could climb on top.
It will be
a strong foundation.
So is Jesus.
When he steps in my path,
I will not go around him,
I will not look for treasure.
I will not chisel it away,
but I will claim him as my foundation!
Praise you, Lord, for Jesus,
our true foundation!
Amen!

"But where can wisdom be found? And where is the place of understanding?"

—Job 28:12

God of all Wisdom,
I spent my life searching
for wisdom from
other people,
books,
literature,
education,
within myself.
I searched for understanding of this world
in the same places.
I can learn facts,
obtain knowledge.
I can read all that others have written,
and not have wisdom!
You are the only source
of real wisdom and understanding.
I humble myself before you, wonderful Lord!
Through Jesus Christ,
Amen.

"When your fathers tested Me, they tried Me though they had seen My work."

—Psalms 95: 9

My glorious Lord,
I see your work in all the world,
in the green grasses,
the colorful flowers,
each tree that grows,
each bird that flies.
Your work is all around me!
I praise you for your creation!
How could I test you more
than to study the amazing way
you have created all things on earth?
I see your glory in all mankind;
each one is different.
You have made us all as you desired;
we are perfect in your eyes.
You love us all,
each with a purpose here on earth.
You desire for all to be saved!
Thank you, Lord, for loving me
as much as you love the flowers and the birds!
I praise you, Lord, through Jesus,
Amen.

"Tekel: You have been weighed on the scales and found deficient."

—Daniel 5:27

My God, you found Belshazzar deficient.
He did not humble himself before you,
did not give you honor.
Then he fell.
You gave him warning by the
handwriting on the wall.
Lord, when have you given me a sign
so plain I did not see it?
Many times, my God!
Sometimes through my arrogance
I misinterpreted it,
and fell into a pit!
When I humbled myself before you,
you strengthened me for the long climb out!
Help me to understand the signs
you give me,
so I will stay on the path
you have for me.
Through Jesus Christ,
Amen!

"I, the Lord, search the heart, I test the mind, even to each man according to his ways, according to the results of his deeds."

—Jeremiah 17:10

O Lord, you know all about me.
You do not judge me by my actions,
but you look into my heart
and see what is there!
For Lord, you know that if I do all good things
just for gain and your approval,
without love in my heart,
then works are nothing.
You know my heart
even better than I do.
You know my motives,
my purpose,
my desire in all I do.
You know my mind and all my thoughts.
You know when I am thinking of you
or of worldly things.
You know if I am being persuaded by the evil one,
even before I do!
Correct me at these times, O my Lord.
Through Jesus Christ,
Amen!

*"He pled the cause of the afflicted and needy; then it was well.
Is that not what it means to know Me?"*

—*Jeremiah 22:16*

Lord above all the heavens and earth,
help me to understand!
Show me
what I need to do
with all you have given me.
You have fed and clothed me,
you have sheltered me,
and yet
there is dissatisfaction in my inner being.
The pain is gnawing away at my soul.
I have heard your command!
I will listen to your prophets!
I will plead the cause of the afflicted!
I will serve you, Lord God of Heaven!
Then I will have peace.
Then joy will fill my soul!
Through Jesus Christ,
Amen!

"God is faithful, through whom you were called into fellowship with His Son, Jesus Christ our Lord."

—*I Corinthians 1:9*

I have heard thy call, my God!
Teach me to follow you completely,
guide my every step,
teach me your Word,
imprint it in my mind!
When a decision is needed about your way,
make it as natural as
red, yellow, and green at a stoplight!
Lord, only in this way will I be able
to follow in your path.
You are the one who can bring to pass
what you want me to do,
the way to walk.
Gracious Lord, I am so grateful.
You are by my side always.
My trust is in you!
Mighty is the Lord, I praise you forever!
Through Jesus Christ,
Amen!

"He counts the number of the stars; He gives names to all of them."

—Psalms 147:4

I saw the stars tonight, Lord,
the brilliant lights you made and named.
I saw the stars, Lord,
in all their wondrous glory.
Too many for me to count
against the black velvet sky.
From east to west,
and north to south,
they filled the night sky
with a light so clear and bright,
I was in awe!
If your creation of the stars
fills me with wonder and awe,
what will your presence do?
My Lord, my God,
you are so much greater
than all your creations together!
I praise you, my Creator.
Through Jesus,
Amen.

"For a child will be born to us, a son will be given to us; and the government will rest on His shoulders; and His name will be called Wonderful Counselor."

—*Isaiah 9:6*

Holy Lord, long before Jesus came to earth as a baby,
you told Isaiah of his coming.
Your all-knowing love knew how weak man was,
and you planned a way to save us from
the evil one.
At the right time,
you would send your son;
not to rule,
but to teach us about you,
to be a sacrificial lamb to atone for our sins.
What a wonderful gift you gave to us.
You showed the depth of your love,
how much you desire our salvation,
our companionship,
our love.
Thank you, my God,
you alone I adore!
Through Jesus Christ,
Amen!

"Faithful is He who calls you, and He also will bring it to pass."

Ever faithful Lord!
You are always there, always constant!
Because you are in charge,
I can be sure that the sun will shine each day,
and each night there will be darkness!
The sun's rays you have made to warm me,
to nurture all you have put on the earth.
Though there may be clouds to hide the sun,
we know the sun is in the heavens above.
You bring the clouds to give rain,
the life-giving rains.
So it is in my life; there are clouds,
but if I wait on you, Lord,
there will be blessings falling from them!
You are faithful and your timing is perfect!
I praise you, Lord!
Through your son, Jesus Christ,
Amen!

22 | FEATHER ON THE WATER

"But let all who take refuge in You be glad, let them sing for joy; and may You shelter them, that those who love Your name may exult in You."

—*Psalms 5:11*

My Lord, my God!
Many times when I was going my own way,
on the wrong path,
you deterred me
that I might change my way.
When I listened to your gentle correction,
my path was clear.
You have given me refuge and shelter
from the many storms in my life!
Even when I did not lift my heart
to your loving ways,
you were there
to help me find my way back to you!
I think of Jesus
and how he died for my salvation.
You sent him because you knew
I could not save myself.
He took all my sins and missteps
with him to the cross!
O Lord, I pray that I will not hurt you again!
Through Jesus Christ,
Amen!

"But she came and began to bow down before Him, saying, 'Lord, help me!'"

—Matthew 15:25

I need you,
my almighty Lord!
I need you,
my gracious God,
that I may see the way to go.
I need you,
my faithful Lord,
to lead me.
I need you,
my creator God!
Help me, Lord, to honor your name
and fulfill your plan.
Without your help, I can do nothing;
you are my strength, my life.
Lord, help me.
Through your son, Jesus Christ,
Amen!

"... but let it be the hidden person of the heart, with the imperishable quality of a gentle and quiet spirit, which is precious in the sight of God."

—*I Peter 3:4*

My Father, you see deeply into my heart.
Nothing is hidden from you!
You see me clearly.
When I am quiet and listen,
I know you are with me.
I must shut out all things of this world,
all the cares,
all the voices,
all the trials!
Then only you will be in my heart.
Thank you, Lord, for being with me
in the quiet, still times.
I will keep you in my heart
that I may have your peace always,
though the world may be tumbling about me.
Thank you, Lord.
Through Jesus Christ,
Amen!

"The sacrifices of God are a broken spirit; a broken and a contrite heart, O God, You will not despise."

—Psalms 51:17

Lord, you have created all things.
How could I build anything to honor you?
All I have came from you, Lord,
and belongs to you still.
To sacrifice what you have given to me
would only be giving back what is already yours!
I can give you the freedom you gave me.
I will give you my heart;
I will be contrite.
I will allow my strong spirit to be broken for you,
to give up my pride,
my confidence,
and allow myself to be weak.
O Lord, you do not despise my weakness
when I give myself to your hands.
You will replace it with your strength.
Praise the Lord!
Amen!

"I will sing to the Lord, because He has dealt bountifully with me."

—Psalms 13:6

My precious God, my Lord and Savior,
what a joy to open my eyes in the morning
and see all the wonderful things
you have surrounded me with!
All is from you!
I see the tall, straight tree
that will give beauty and shade for many years;
a shelter and home
to many birds and small creatures.
Even the insects
you cover with many brilliant colors!
They are food for other creatures.
All is in perfect balance!
When my life is out of balance,
I remember this.
I know that you are in control,
I rest in peace,
Lord Jesus,
Amen!

"And in your lovingkindness, cut off my enemies and destroy all those who afflict my soul, for I am Your servant."

—*Psalms 143:12*

Humble me, Lord,
that I may be your servant.
Give me grace to serve you
in my daily walk.
Make me a servant, Lord,
to all I meet.
Put before me those
you desire me to serve.
In loving others,
I will sow my love for you!
I will serve the lowly,
the sick,
the helpless,
the poor,
the prisoner,
the repressed.
You love them all, Lord,
you desire to have all come to you!
Through Jesus Christ,
Amen!

"From His dwelling place He looks out on all the inhabitants of the earth."

—*Psalms 33:14*

You are looking out for me, Lord!
You will watch over me
and supply all my needs.
You, Lord, know of my struggles,
my pain, my loss.
I praise you, my Lord God, in Heaven.
You are so wonderful to care for me.
I cannot comprehend the expanse of
your love and your power,
yet it is there!
My heart rejoices knowing
you are always with me.
You have my back!
Thank you, Lord.
Through Jesus,
Amen!

"It will also come to pass that before they call, I will answer; and while they are still speaking, I will hear."

—*Isaiah 65:24*

My Heavenly Father,
with a grateful heart, I come to you.
You are all-good and all-knowing.
You have cared for me all my life.
You have answered my prayers,
you have answered my unasked prayers.
You alone knew what I needed
all of my yesterdays,
even before I knew!
You alone know what I need today.
You already have answered
all my prayers of tomorrow.
While your answers, Lord,
are not always what I expect,
what I receive is superior to what I ask for!
My precious Lord and Savior,
I praise you and your greatness,
your constant love and kindness,
your all-knowing Spirit.
I pray through your son, Jesus,
Amen!

"In the beginning God created the heavens and the earth."

—*Genesis 1:1*

Lord God,
you have created everything.
We are so excited when we create
or discover something.
But in essence,
you are the one who has created all of this.
Our ability to create has
come from you, O Lord.
You have put this ability and
the ideas into our minds.
It is your creativity that we see
in solving a problem,
or in being artistic.
You have created all that we have to work with.
Lord, you have gifted mankind
to use your creations
to produce everything we do.
Praise to you, Lord!
Through your son we pray,
Amen!

"Now I have told you before it happens, so that when it happens, you may believe."

—*John 14:29*

Precious Jesus,
you told the disciples
you would die and rise again,
that they, and I, may believe that what you say
will come to pass.
Holy Spirit, you have often given me
"nudges" about things in my life.
I believe that you have done this
so when these events came to pass
I would believe.
Lord, my faith has been increased by these times.
I will listen for your messages,
and know that you will be true to them.
Thank you, Lord, for your constant
kindness and patience
in guiding me to deeper faith in you.
Praise be to Jesus,
Amen!

". . . as God has allotted to each a measure of faith."

—Romans 12:3

Glorious Lord,
whenever I feel my faith is not strong enough
to carry me through a difficult time,
I think of this verse.
How much faith is enough?
How big is the "measure" you gave us?
I believe that if we needed more,
you would have given it to us!
Faith as small as a mustard seed is all we need
if we believe and use it!
It is not the size of our faith
but how deep our belief.
You have given me all the faith I need.
Thank you, Lord,
for always caring for me,
for giving me all that I need to follow you!
Through Jesus Christ,
Amen!

"And let the rough ground become a plain, and the rugged terrain a broad valley."

—*Isaiah 40:4*

O Lord, my God,
my shepherd!
There are times I think,
Oh, if you would only make all rugged areas
of my life smooth!
What would I be
if you would grant this to me?
Exercise strengthens my body,
difficulties strengthen my faith.
Lord, if life was easy,
I would soon stop depending on you!
What meaning would life have
if I did not need you?
Thank you, Lord, for giving me the exercise
to be strong
so I can do the work
you have for me to do here on earth.
I praise you, my shepherd,
who will guide me through all the rough and rugged terrain
until I get to the valley of rest!
Through Jesus Christ,
Amen!

"Brethren, I do not regard myself as having laid hold of it yet; but one thing I do: forgetting what lies behind and reaching forward to what lies ahead."

—Philippians 3:13

My Lord, my God,
at times I forget that you
have forgiven all my sins and mistakes of the past;
then I end up dwelling on them!
This only hinders what
you have for me to do in the future.
Lord, I know there is much to do
to make myself righteous for you.
I pray for guidance from the Holy Spirit
to help me continue striving for this goal!
I know that I am being guided,
step by step, to the eternal life
given to us by Jesus.
When I surrender all my life to Jesus,
I am in good hands and know that
you will never forsake me!
Praise the Lord!
Through Jesus Christ,
Amen!

PRAISE AND THANKS

When my heart is low, five minutes of praising in word and song lifts my spirit and brings joy to my heart!

When I awake in the morning and the sun is shining, I thank the Lord. When it is raining or cloudy, I thank the Lord! I enjoy praising and thanking God for all things, whether it is something I want or not. I know that he sends me what I need, and sometimes my circumstances are not exactly what I asked for! As Job said in Job 2:10, "Shall we indeed accept good from God but not accept adversity?"

Praising and thanking the Lord for all things has a powerful effect on my heart. When I thank the Lord for less-than-desirable circumstances, stress melts away, because I am acknowledging that God is in control. This gives me a wonderful feeling of peace. He is with me!

I don't believe God sends painful things our way to hurt or punish us. I believe that he allows them to happen to teach us through both direct and indirect consequences to sin. God loves us and wants what is best for us! He can take the toughest situations and turn them around for good. That is worth giving praise and thanks!

"The heavens are Yours, the earth also is Yours. The world and all it contains, You have founded them."

—Psalms 89:11

My precious creator,
as I look into the heavens,
I see how great you are!
You have made the warmth of the sun,
and the blue of the sky!
At night, I see the brilliant moon
light the heavens,
an angel
guiding me through the darkness!
The stars, so far away,
yet I feel I could reach out
and hold them in my hand!
You have a plan for all the universe.
You have a plan for me!
O thank you, Lord.
Amen!

"'For I know the plans that I have for you,' declares the Lord."

—*Jeremiah 29:11*

Praise the Lord!
You care so much and have a plan for me!
How wonderful it is that you will guide me
in the ways that please you!
I will listen closely for your words,
I will surrender to you,
I will watch constantly for you, Lord,
so I will not miss the path.
Knowing you are with me
increases my desire to please you,
to live for you, Lord!
I praise you, my God,
with a grateful heart!
Glory to you forever!
Through Jesus Christ I pray,
Amen!

"Give us this day our daily bread."

—Matthew 6:11

Heavenly Father,
you are so faithful to care for me.
Jesus taught us how to pray
for all that is necessary to be your child.
My daily bread is much more than what I eat.
It is spiritual nourishment for my soul!
It is the life-giving water!
The words of this prayer
encompass all that I need to remember
to serve you,
to be close to you,
to be with you in eternity!
Thank you, Jesus!
Amen!

"O give thanks to the Lord, for He is good; for His lovingkindness is everlasting."

—I Chronicles 16:34

I lift my eyes to the heavens!
I praise you, Heavenly Father,
for all good things come from you!
I know you hear me when I call.
Thank you for caring for me!
Teach me to ask for things
that will help me grow spiritually,
to further your work
here on earth.
Serving you is my one desire.
You will give me all that I need to serve you!
Abundantly, you have given to me.
May my gratitude be abundant also!
Through Jesus Christ,
Amen!

"I will give thanks to the Lord with all my heart; I will tell of all Your wonders. I will be glad and exult in You, I will sing praise to Your name, O Most High."

—*Psalms 9:1–2*

Yes, my Lord, I praise you for all my world!
Each day, mighty God,
you deserve my praise and thankfulness!
I thank you for trials.
They are so small compared to the ways
I have hurt you.
You have given me strength
to overcome all things!
Thank you for your faithfulness
in being with me always!
You alone, O God, give me all I need;
you love me unconditionally.
You gave your precious son, Jesus,
to die for me,
for I am unable to save myself.
I pray that the whole world will praise you
and give thanks to you
for your wonderful lovingkindness!
Through Jesus Christ,
Amen!

"Well done, good and faithful slave. You were faithful with a few things, I will put you in charge of many things."

—*Matthew 25:23*

Father in Heaven,
I pray that by following your way,
I will bring honor to you during my life on earth!
I pray that the expectations for myself
will not be lower
than what you have planned for me.
Make known to me, my God,
the path you have set before me.
Even though the tasks seem menial in my eyes,
it is your desire, and,
therefore, noble!
I pray I will be faithful in the small things
so that I will please you.
You are the only one I adore!
Through Jesus Christ,
Amen!

"The Levites, their relatives, had charge of the treasures of the house of God and of the treasures of the dedicated gifts."

—*I Chronicles 26:20*

I also have charge of the many gifts
you have given to me, my God.
Not treasures of gold and jewels, but of Jesus,
the Holy Spirit, and my salvation!
They are worth far more than any treasure on earth!
Yet, I sometimes take them for granted,
and do not show my gratitude
for such great gifts.
Without Jesus, we would
not have salvation.
O Lord, I do need the Holy Spirit to guide me
in all my paths.
You have done all these things
that we may have eternal life.
I will hold these gifts in my heart
and remember them all my days.
Praise be to you, my God.
Through Jesus,
Amen!

"Your Father knows what you need before you ask Him."

—Matthew 6:8

My perfect, wonderful Lord,
each day you show me something
to be thankful for,
to learn from,
to display your faithfulness!
May I learn what you have for me today!
Lord, you carried me through difficult times.
Grant me the grace, Lord,
to show others the way to you.
Help me be patient,
show unconditional love,
respect, and kindness
to all I meet,
as you have shown me!
I praise you, Lord!
Through Jesus Christ,
Amen!

"In peace I will both lie down and sleep, for You alone, O Lord, make me to dwell in safety."

—*Psalms 4:8*

O Lord, when sleep eludes me, I repeat this verse.
When I roll restlessly,
and my mind is filled with thoughts
of failure, finances,
dangers, disasters, loved ones—
you are there!
Your calm comes;
I rest with you in my heart.
My heart fills with peace and thanksgiving.
I know that I am loved.
Then sleep comes!
Your words, O Lord, give my heart peace
when all about me is in turmoil.
Peace, peace, true peace comes only from you!
Thank you, my God,
for this wonderful gift that fills me to bursting.
I will praise you, Lord, forever and ever.
I lift my hands to you, I bow down to you.
You have given me your Word!
Through Jesus,
Amen!

"Remember His wonders which He has done, His marvels and the judgments uttered by His mouth."

—Psalms 105:5

Almighty God of Heaven and earth,
of all the universe!
Your wonders are all around me!
Wherever I look, there are your wonders,
from the highest heavens
to the inner part of the earth!
You have made mankind in your image,
the child, the man, the woman,
the lowly, the high,
the poor, the wealthy,
the sinners, the holy ones,
the weak, the strong.
They are all yours!
The wonders you have done through the ages
I will remember, Lord.
They show me you are always with me.
Your judgments are perfect!
Thank you, my Lord.
Through Jesus,
Amen!

"Just as I have been with Moses, I will be with you; I will not fail you or forsake you."

—*Joshua 1:5*

My wonderful Lord and God,
you are always with me.
You have cared for me
when I did not care for myself.
You have loved me
when I did not love myself.
You have shown me the path
to the way out of my darkness.
You are always faithful,
you have never left me.
I only need to ask, and you are here.
Although I am not worthy,
you sent your son for my salvation
to make me worthy!
You have given me so many gifts!
How can I not praise you day and night?
Through Jesus Christ,
Amen!

"…and He died for all, so that they who live might no longer live for themselves, but for Him who died and rose again on their behalf."

—II Corinthians 5:15

My Jesus,
you did it for me!
Yes, you did it for me!
You took my greed,
my unkind acts,
my hates,
my unkind words,
my laziness,
my neglect of your Father,
my selfishness,
my lusts,
and took them into your heart.
With your heart breaking, you went to the cross
and took all my sins with you,
so I could have salvation!
Precious Jesus, how can I give you thanks?
I will honor your name!
I will keep my Father in my heart at all times!
I will bow to you in gratitude,
I will tell others of your great love!
I adore you, Jesus,
Amen!

"Do not fear or be dismayed because of this great multitude, for the battle is not yours but God's."

—*II Chronicles 20:15*

O praise the Holy God;
he battles for me
on this earthly battlefield.
When multitudes of difficulties come my way,
when my mind is confused and dark,
when my eyes are blinded by things of this world,
then I know!
Yes! You are with me to clear my mind,
to be the light,
to be my sight.
O thank you, my precious Savior!
You are my salvation.
You are my guide.
You are my counselor.
You are my friend!
I will praise you forever!
Praise Jesus,
Amen!

"I planted, Apollos watered, but God was causing the growth."

—*I Corinthians 3:6*

I planted a seed today.
I told someone of your work
with the poor and needy.
I have seeded, Lord,
I pray that it fell on rich ground!
May the seed sprout in their heart,
be watered,
grow,
produce fruit,
and spread more seed.
Now, I leave it in your hands,
for I know that you cause the growth!
I praise you, Lord,
for giving me the seed to plant
and a place to plant it!
Through Jesus Christ,
Amen!

"Who shall separate us from the love of Christ? Will tribulation, or distress, or persecution, or famine, or nakedness, or peril, or sword? . . . But in all of these things we overwhelmingly conquer through Him who loved us."

—Romans 8:35, 37

Heavenly Father,
I know that you are with me always,
yet today my heart is heavy.
Sad thoughts fill my mind;
if only I had a cave to crawl into!
Instead, my God, I choose to think of your glory!
Lift my heart, Lord,
as you have done so many times!
Awaken in my mind
the joy in serving you.
In spite of the heaviness of my heart,
give me the words of love to say
so others may know you!
Make my eyes see the beauty
that surrounds me!
You are everywhere, precious Lord!
Through Jesus Christ,
Amen!

"Give thanks to the God of gods, for His lovingkindness is everlasting."

—*Psalms 136:2*

My perfect, wonderful Lord!
Each moment you show me something to be
thankful for,
to learn from.
You show me your faithfulness!
Some things are seen,
others not seen.
May I learn what you have for me today;
you have something special for each person!
Help me learn patience
that I might show the unconditional love,
respect,
and kindness to others
that you have shown me!
I am in your arms!
Through Jesus Christ,
Amen!

"Thus let all Your enemies perish, O Lord; but let those who love Him be like the rising of the sun in its might..."

—*Judges 5:31*

My God, the sun shines its wonderful rays
down on us
bringing us warmth and beauty!
I pray that as the sun shines
and brings life to this world
that you, O Lord,
will send many warm blessings to those I love:
my family, my friends, my country, and the world!
Shine down upon all!
Heal hearts and minds!
Fill me with love for every being!
Your sun shines over all the earth.
Everyone can partake of its benefits.
May each ray be felt as a blessing from you!
You are the Eternal Light!
I praise you,
through your son, Jesus,
Amen!

"Seek the Lord and His strength; seek His face continually."

—*Psalms 105:4*

O, my God, you are beautiful!
May I see your face forever before me,
in the sunrise,
in the sunset,
and all day long!
Help me to think of you continuously!
You are in all things,
for you have made all things.
You have created me,
therefore, you are in me!
Lord, how can I ever feel unloved,
alone, or abandoned?
I only need to call out to you
to seek your face!
Then there is peace and comfort;
loneliness is gone.
I am loved by you!
Your only desire is for me to love you, my Lord.
Thank you,
through your son, Jesus,
Amen!

"There is no fear in love; but perfect love casts out fear, because fear involves punishment, and the one who fears is not perfected in love."

—*I John 4:18*

O, my loving God!
There is none like you.
I am not afraid to have you near,
in my heart,
for you love me as only you can!
Your love is perfect!
I shall remember this always.
I will tell others of your wonders,
to call on you
for protection and guidance.
You only will I adore!
I will shout it to the world!
Through Jesus,
Amen!

"In everything give thanks; for this is God's will for you in Christ Jesus."

—*I Thessalonians 5:18*

My Lord and my God,
accept my gratitude for all things in my life!
I thank you for the warm sunshine,
for days of clouds and cold,
for the nights that I sleep in peace,
and for the sleepless ones!
Thank you for all the people I meet,
especially for those who do not know your love.
May they see you through me!
Thank you for health
and times of sickness.
Thank you for well-being
and times of pain.
Thank you for good relationships
and times of heartbreak.
I call on you,
I surrender all to you,
that you may carry me!
Through Jesus Christ,
Amen!

"And my God will supply all your needs according to His riches in glory in Christ Jesus."

—*Philippians 4:19*

What shall I give to you, my God?
The whole world is yours!
You have created all that is in it.
I have only what you have allowed me to use.
It is all yours, Lord!
I will use it for your work,
for your plan.
You have given me all I need
to show others my love for you,
for I am your servant, O Lord.
I serve others in your name.
With you within my heart, others will see
the joy only you can give.
Through Jesus Christ,
Amen!

"This is the day which the Lord has made; let us rejoice and be glad in it."

— *Psalms 118:24*

What a beautiful day, Lord!
Even before I know if
the sun is shining,
it is cloudy,
or cold,
or rainy,
my first thought is of you.
It is a beautiful day!
When I start the day with you,
it is good!
Lord, I lift my hands to you in joy!
I sing praises to you.
How wonderful you are!
Blessings are all around me,
for you have created it all!
The birds sing angel songs!
The budding trees are like lace against the blue sky!
I see Christ in people,
your most special creation.
Thank you, Lord, for all
the world you have made!
Through Jesus Christ,
Amen!

"I will give thanks to you, for I am fearfully and wonderfully made. Wonderful are Your works, and my soul knows it very well."

—*Psalms 139:14*

O my great and mighty Lord,
you created man in your own image,
and there are so many images to see!
You have made each person unique
in appearance, thoughts, words, and deeds.
Lord, I pray I will see
all these differences
as your handiwork.
We are all equal in your eyes.
Jesus died for everyone,
that all may be saved!
The abilities and gifts I have,
you have given me.
I pray that I will use them for your glory
and not frivolous, worldly things.
My wonderful Lord, I praise you forever!
Through your son, Jesus,
Amen!

"Let me dwell in Your tent forever; let me take refuge in the shelter of Your wings."

—Psalms 61:4

Lord, as I look into the branches
of the old cottonwood tree,
I feel your sheltering arms protecting me
from all harm.
Have you designed these beautiful trees
to remind us of you?
To feel your closeness and protection?
Your sheltering arms
are such a comfort to me.
I am always safe from the cares of this world
when I allow you
to stretch your arms around me!
As the mother bird
stretches her wings around her babies,
I know that you are protecting me with your arms.
I may not see them,
but I can feel your comfort and warmth!
Through Jesus Christ,
Amen!

"He put a new song in my mouth, a song of praise to our God . . ."

—*Psalms 40:3*

O Lord, how blessed I am!
You have taken my cares
upon your shoulders
and replaced them with a song of joy and praise!
My burden is so much lighter
when I share it with you.
Often, I do not wait
for you to fix things,
but hold on so tightly to my problems
that you cannot do your work.
Precious Jesus, when I hand them over to you,
and do not grab them back,
indeed,
you put a song in my heart
and a skip in my walk!
I praise you, Lord, for your Word
and for all your promises.
You are faithful,
you are truth,
only you are worthy of adoration!
Praise your Holy Name.
Through Jesus Christ,
Amen!

". . . that all the peoples of the earth may know that the hand of the Lord is mighty, so that you may fear the Lord your God forever."

—*Joshua 4:24*

Yes, mighty is the hand of the Lord!
He is above all the universe.
He commands the heavens, stars,
moons, and planets!
Therefore, I praise my Lord for all he has created.
How can we question the Lord
in his plans and works?
He is perfect in all ways,
and knows all I do and say.
My wonderful Father,
nothing is hidden from you!
For this I am grateful!
I dearly love you, God of Heaven and earth.
You know what is in my heart!
Glory forever to God!
Through Jesus,
Amen!

"... Father, hallowed be Your name ..."

—*Luke 11:2*

My Lord, such a simple statement,
yet so powerful!
May your name be revered
over all the earth with joy!
May your praises be sung with pure joy and love!
Only you are worthy of our adoration!
I surrender to you, my God,
for that is the only way
I can be sure of following you
all the rest of my days!
When I have praised you
and asked you for a map to follow,
you said, "Follow me."
You are my beloved,
you are my inspiration,
you are my life!
Through Jesus Christ,
Amen!

"My presence shall go with you, and I will give you rest."

—*Exodus 33:14*

Thank you, Lord, for I know
that as you were with the Israelites,
you are with me.
You led them through their journey
with guidance and protection.
I reach for your hand, Lord,
to lead me through the trials in this world.
In your presence
I will rest and be satisfied!
My God, my God, how wonderful you are!
In the daylight, you are near;
in the darkness, you are there!
Even though I cannot see you,
your presence gives me comfort.
I will praise you always!
Glory to the Lord, through Jesus Christ,
Amen!

HEALING BODY AND SOUL

We all desire to be strong and healthy. When we are sick, we want to be healed! When our hearts are broken, we want them put back together! God heals sick bodies and broken hearts!

Sometimes it is our soul that needs healing. If we are unable to feel joy and peace or accept painful situations in our lives, it may be that our soul is in distress. Our wonderful Lord can heal souls, too! God, through the Holy Spirit, has healed my soul. He has been faithful to me and he will be faithful to you also!

We can have salvation with an imperfect body or a hurting heart, but the soul must be healed in order for us to fully experience God's great love and forgiveness.

Praise the Lord that when our souls are healthy, we are able to deal with broken hearts and bodies.

"Surely our griefs He Himself bore, and our sorrows He carried. . . ."

—*Isaiah 53:4*

My Lord,
you have brought me
out of the depths of grief.
You have sustained me,
I praise you for this!
You have shown me
there is life to live after a grievous loss.
In you I will have peace and joy—
yes, even joy!
You will keep me on an even keel;
all I need do is accept that you
are with me and in me.
Thank you, Lord, for never forsaking me,
even when I do not call on you.
I feel the warmth of your presence,
the comfort of your peace.
I will praise you always, my Lord, my God.
Through Jesus Christ,
Amen!

"Then you will call, and the Lord will answer; you will cry, and he will say, 'Here I am. . . .'"

—*Isaiah 58:9*

Praise the Lord, for he hears our cry!
In the wilderness of life,
he is there!
When I am in despair,
he is there!
Why should I feel despair
when the Lord is so close?
Why should I feel lost
when the Lord knows where I am?
I will call to the Lord through
my pain
and emptiness.
He will hear me and heal my heart!
There is only joy
when I surrender to the Lord!
Praise him! Praise him!
Through Jesus,
Amen!

"O Lord, my God, I cried to You for help, and You healed me."

—*Psalms 30:2*

Wonderful Lord, you give me life;
you heal me!
What a wonderful Savior you are!
Each morning,
I thank you anew
for these gifts!
I give you my life and all that I do.
All day, I think of you and your wonders!
At night, I praise you before I sleep!
There is not a day that I do not think of the wonders
you have made!
Lord, my body is weak and defenseless
against the disease of this world.
I lean on Jesus to protect me,
for he knows what temptations
I face each day.
I listen for your voice in all I do.
I believe that you are always there,
waiting for me to listen.
Thank you Father, Son, and Holy Spirit,
Amen!

"It is I who put to death and give life. I have wounded and it is I who heal. . . ."

—*Deuteronomy 32:39*

Lord God, Almighty,
you have the power over life and death.
When a loved one is ill or dies, I ask why?
I want to have some say in this
to be able to help them.
Lord, you have a reason for everything.
Death is difficult to accept, to think about.
I miss my loved ones.
I want to keep them always.
However, that is your decision alone.
In your care, they have joy and peace.
I give you complete control
over my life and those whom I love.
All healing comes through you.
Heal my grief, Lord,
give me peace.
Thank you, Lord,
Amen!

"And Moses cried out to the Lord, saying, 'O God, heal her, I pray!'"

—Numbers 12:13

My Lord, my God!
When Moses cried out for Miriam,
she needed spiritual healing.
Many times, I do not realize
how much I need spiritual healing
and fail to ask for it,
not allowing you to heal me.
Failing to accept my need for it
can become a boulder in my path!
It can bring me down in body, mind, and heart!
Help me, Lord, to see this in myself
when the need arises.
Teach me, O Lord, to ask for forgiveness
and to forgive others.
Then I may feel your joy in my heart
and be lifted up to you in many ways.
My heart will be lighter,
the climb will be slighter,
the view more beautiful!
Thank you, O Lord, for teaching me forgiveness;
thank you for forgiving me!
Through Jesus,
Amen!

"So he got up and came to his father. But while he was a long way off, his father saw him and felt compassion for him, and ran and embraced him and kissed him."

—Luke 15:20

Lord, I think back
to all the wonderful healing
you have done in my life!
The most precious is healed relationships
of family and friends.
What a wonderful gift you gave!
These relationships you continue to bless.
My relationship with you
is so precious,
so meaningful.
I pray you will guide me through the steps
of reconciliation with all
I have had conflict with!
Prepare me for the renewal of love
as you prepared the father and the prodigal son!
Only through you can this be done!
Your love can heal any broken situation.
Bless my relationships, Lord.
I praise you forever!
Through Jesus Christ,
Amen!

"Yet it is I who taught Ephraim to walk; I took them in My arms, but they did not know that I healed them."

—*Hosea 11:3*

How many times, O Lord,
have you walked with me
or held me up when I could not stand,
and I did not know that it was you
who carried me along?
How many times, O Lord,
have you healed me of pain and sorrow,
and I did not give you a thought?
Lord God, now I know that it was you!
You have been by my side all these years,
helping, guiding, healing, carrying me.
Forgive me, Lord, and heal my heart.
Never let me forget that it is you who cares for me!
Even when I do not think of you,
you are there!
Through Jesus Christ,
Amen!

"But Jesus, turning and seeing her, said, 'Daughter, take courage, your faith has made you well.'"

—*Matthew 9:22*

Precious Jesus,
you did not withhold yourself from people
but gave of your strength and power
for their good.
Thank you, Jesus!
You gave your life for my salvation,
and still give so much of your power and love
to all who come to you,
trust you, and believe in you.
You heal hearts,
minds,
souls,
bodies.
O wonderful Savior, I bow before you
for only you are worthy of adoration.
Praise to you, Jesus,
Amen!

". . . and they brought to Him all who were ill, those suffering with various diseases and pains, demoniacs, epileptics, paralytics; and He healed them."

—Matthew 4:24

God is the same yesterday, today, and tomorrow.
Jesus healed many while he was on earth.
He heals people yet today.
My Lord and my God,
perhaps the healing is not accomplished
as it was when you walked the earth.
You have given the world
many medical treatments today,
yet the healing still comes from you!
Just as a seed cannot sprout
without your intervention,
healing cannot happen without your help.
I pray, Lord, that those who are ill
will give their lives over to you
so you can heal them in the way
you know best for them!
Through Jesus,
Amen!

"But the centurion said, 'Lord, I am not worthy for You to come under my roof, but just say the word, and my servant will be healed.'"

—Matthew 8:8

Lord, the centurion said
he was not worthy
to have Jesus come under his roof—
none of us are worthy.
We are incapable of making ourselves worthy!
Only your grace gives us that privilege!
Yet, you come under our roof, into our bodies,
to save us, and to heal us.
Your unconditional love
is too great for us to comprehend!
I praise you, my God,
I thank you, my God.
You have desired for me to be close to you,
to be healed by you.
Lord Almighty,
I could never be worthy by myself.
Jesus died so that we can be accepted by you.
To you, all praise and glory,
Amen!

". . . for I, the Lord, am your healer."

—*Exodus 15:26*

Almighty God,
since the days of Moses
you have declared yourself the master healer!
Then you sent Jesus, your son,
to heal many during his days on earth.
In your Word,
we are encouraged to pray for healing.
Lord, when we pray according to your will,
you hear our prayers.
If we do not believe that you can heal,
then why pray for it?
We pray for physical, emotional,
mental, and spiritual healing.
Lord, I put the spiritual healing first.
Then my heart will be pure;
I will understand what you want for me.
I trust you, Lord, to care for my physical body.
I accept your will for me.
Thank you. Through Jesus Christ,
Amen!

"Shall we indeed accept good from God and not accept adversity?"

—Job 2:10

When will I know, Lord?
When will I know you have healed me
spiritually,
emotionally,
physically?
I know you answer prayer, Lord.
Sometimes yes, sometimes no,
sometimes wait awhile.
When will I know?
I take my mustard seed of faith
and use it in prayer.
I can be healed in any way you desire.
I just need to accept whatever happens
as your answer!
I need to claim my healing
even when I do not feel it is done.
I will know I am where you want me to be.
By praying sincerely,
and accepting my situation as your will,
I have peace!
Through Jesus Christ,
Amen!

"He said, 'I am God, the God of your father; do not be afraid to go down to Egypt, for I will make you a great nation there.'"

—*Genesis 46:3*

Lord, you said, "Do not be afraid to go down to Egypt."
Do you have an "Egypt" for me?
Is it next door?
Across town?
Far away?
Perhaps my Egypt is right here.
I am listening, Lord.
I will listen each day
for the Holy Spirit to tell me
where you want me to go.
I am willing, Lord, to do the smallest,
lowest work you have for me.
Bringing your Word to others
is noble work.
Make me worthy, Lord, to repeat your Word.
Praise to you, Lord,
for your wonderful plan of salvation.
Make me worthy, Lord!
Through Jesus,
Amen!

"Woe to him who builds his house without righteousness."

—*Jeremiah 22:13*

My Lord and Father,
you created everything
for our blessings and enjoyment.
I have used these things for my own
glory, gain, and comfort,
without thanking you for all.
If I do not use them to serve my family,
friends, and neighbors,
I will not be blessed by you!
O Lord of Righteousness, heal me from any desires
to use all this for my own gain and glory.
Keep from me the afflictions of the uncaring,
the unbelieving,
those who do not serve you.
Forgive me, Lord,
that my heart may be healed.
Through Jesus Christ,
Amen!

"The Lord will sustain him on his sickbed; in his illness, You restore him to health."

—*Psalms 41:3*

Lord, my Sustenance, my Healer!
So many times
you have healed my heart,
my soul, my body!
O, mighty God, I have joy
because you are with me!
Once again, Lord, I need your healing hand!
I writhe in pain within that only you can see.
Heal me, Lord, in any way that you see fit.
I rejoice in your wonderful love
and understanding!
Heal me according to your will
and wonderful grace!
Your presence gives me strength to endure.
I will praise you forever.
Through Jesus Christ,
Amen!

"I have heard your prayer, I have seen your tears; behold, I will heal you."

—2 Kings 20:5

Hezekiah prayed to you, O Lord.
You answered his prayer and healed him.
So many times you have heard my prayers,
seen my tears,
and have blessed me!
How can I thank you, my God,
for hearing my prayers and pleas to you?
Wonderful, glorious Lord,
you care so much for me,
you take away the pain of my heart and soul;
you heal me.
It is beyond my understanding!
I praise you; I come to you in gratitude.
Forgive me for times I have hurt you
and walked away from you.
Lord Jesus, the pain you endured on the cross
was caused by my sins.
There is none like you!
Praise to Jesus,
Amen!

"Heal me, O Lord, and I will be healed; save me and I will be saved, for You are my praise."

—*Jeremiah 17:14*

Almighty God,
you and you alone will I adore!
You are mighty to save me when I come to you.
I am humbled before you!
I plead for forgiveness of my sins!
Lead me in the way you have set for me.
You have been faithful all my life.
You will be faithful for my remaining days!
I pray I will remain faithful to you,
not straying from your path.
Then you can heal me: body, soul, and spirit.
O Lord, to spend eternity with you is my desire.
I know at that time, I will be whole,
my body will be perfect.
You will heal me.
I adore you, only you!
Through Jesus,
Amen!

"A time to kill and a time to heal; a time to tear down and time to build up."

—Ecclesiastes 3:3

All things come in your time.
When I ask for healing,
you heal me according to your plan!
You rebuild my health
when you know it is the right time.
You rebuild my heart
when you know it is ready.
Lord, sometimes you choose not to heal,
but I know that I will be whole in Heaven,
my body will be as new!
Lord, I pray that I will use my time in illness,
healing, and being rebuilt to praise you!
I worship you, Heavenly Father,
for you know what is best for me!
When I turn to you and listen,
all you say is good.
I shall follow you forever!
I will tell the world of your wonderful works!
Through Jesus Christ,
Amen!

TEMPTATION AND FORGIVENESS

It says in I Corinthians 10:13 that all are tempted. The evil one is devious and very charming in his desire to drag us away from our Lord. Often we are tempted without realizing that Satan has a grip on us. Even then, it is not too late to call for help! God will help us when we are tempted and give us the strength to pull away from Satan.

"All have sinned" (Romans 3:23). Sinning is doing something displeasing and hurtful to God. Jesus died to cleanse us from our sins so we can enjoy forgiveness and eternal life in Heaven (I John 1:9). God knows what is in our hearts! He is faithful and will forgive us when we sincerely repent and ask for forgiveness.

As God models forgiveness to us, we must also forgive when someone has offended us. Sometimes, I have to forgive a person many times before I can feel the lasting forgiveness in my heart. This is human nature. Many times, praying for the person has brought me to a place where I am willing and able to forgive him or her. With each temptation and moment of forgiveness, we become stronger in the Lord!

"It was for freedom that Christ set us free; therefore keep standing firm and do not be subject again to a yoke of slavery."

—*Galatians 5:1*

Wonderful Lord Jesus, who set me free,
every day I will praise you.
You have given me freedom from
bondage to sin,
bondage to my past,
bondage to disbelief!
The evil one likes nothing better
than to have me believe I am in his control!
Satan put me in bondage
to a selfish desire,
a mistake from the past.
He kept me a slave to guilt!
Then I saw what the evil one had done.
I asked Jesus Christ to break the bondage,
and I broke free with Jesus!
O, thank you, Jesus,
for breaking the bond of slavery
to the things of this world!
I cannot praise you enough!
Praise Jesus! Praise Jesus!
Praise the Lord God Almighty!
Amen.

"But if you do not forgive, neither will your Father who is in heaven forgive your transgressions."

—Mark 11:26

Praise to the Lord
who is ever faithful.
When I ask, Lord, you will make known to me
each part of my life that I need to improve.
Lord, I pray you will bring to mind
each person
that I need to forgive.
Then I will forgive each one.
Help me to remember that each person
is precious in your eyes.
I want to see others as you do.
Only in this way will I be clean,
able to come to you for forgiveness.
You are so faithful, Lord,
to forgive when we forgive others!
Thank you, Lord.
Through Jesus,
Amen!

"I am the Lord your God; you shall not fear the gods of the Amorites in whose land you live. But you have not obeyed Me."

—Judges 6:10

My Lord,
you are the God that spoke to Gideon
when the people of Israel hid in dens in Midian.
You speak the same words today.
Today's gods may not be
statues and altars
for worship and sacrifice.
They are more subtle and devious.
These are gods of materialism,
gods of pleasure,
gods of self-indulgence,
gods of comfort!
They try to lure me in every way!
I do not fear, my Almighty God,
I trust you to defeat them;
they will not have power over me.
O Lord, I will remember you
and keep your Word in my heart;
then these other gods will be destroyed.
Through Jesus Christ,
Amen!

"Rest in the Lord and wait patiently for Him."

—Psalms 37:7

My Lord and my God,
when I am restless and anxious,
I will remember these words!
You will be with me and help me rest in you.
Though it may seem empty ahead,
you have my life all planned out.
You know all about me, you see all I do.
I will listen, Lord, for your voice,
I will search for all your truths.
Your Word calms me;
I can rest in you!
You care for me and will clear the path ahead.
When I listen to you, I will not stumble!
O my Heavenly Father, I praise you
and all you are!
May the whole world praise you!
I pray that all mankind will rejoice in your Word!
Through Jesus Christ,
Amen!

"Satan has demanded permission to sift you like wheat."

—*Luke 22:31*

My mighty and wonderful Lord,
by this verse, I know that Satan's power is limited.
He still needs to ask permission from you, God!
Make me strong,
that I may withstand
the fiery darts of his evil ways.
Then I will be a witness for you
when Satan brings
his temptation before me.
I know that you are by my side!
I want to hear only your voice, my Lord,
to warn, to guide, to protect me
at all times.
You are my one and only guardian,
my Lord!
Through Jesus Christ,
Amen!

"Blessed be the Lord, my rock, who trains my hands for war, and my fingers for battle."

—Psalms 144:1

I do not often think of being in a war.
Yet, I am constantly aware
of the temptations
that draw me away from
what you have planned for me.
I study your Word.
It gives me the tools I need
to overcome the evil one
when he tempts me.
You will teach me to push away
all the things that are not worthy of you.
Thank you, Lord.
Please keep preparing me
for all the new situations
that are put upon me.
Through Jesus Christ,
Amen!

". . . for I will forgive their iniquity, and their sin I will remember no more."

—Jeremiah 31:34

My wonderful Lord,
you not only forgive me,
but then you remember it no more!
Lord, you know all things.
You no longer hold my iniquity against me.
Teach me, Lord, to do the same
for those who have offended me.
Teach me to forgive others,
to start anew in my relationships.
Teach me to love others,
even though I disagree with them.
You made all people unique;
you love all.
Through your example I will love all mankind
for they are your creation!
Through Jesus Christ,
Amen!

"And do not lead us into temptation, but deliver us from evil."

—*Matthew 6:13*

O Lord, if only I would remember
to trust you
to protect me from temptation!
I ask in prayer,
but still doubt
you will deliver me from all evil!
When temptation is difficult to resist,
I only need to call on you!
You, O Lord, will show me the way out!
You will protect me.
Daily, I see temptations around me;
you are there waiting for me to trust you!
Lead me away
from the temptations of the evil one!
Through your son, Jesus,
Amen!

"For Hezekiah prayed for them, saying, 'May the Good Lord pardon everyone who prepares his heart to seek God, the Lord God of his fathers.' . . . So the Lord heard Hezekiah and healed the people."

—*II Chronicles 30:18–20*

O Lord, Great Forgiver,
Hezekiah, your holy man, came to you
in prayer, and you answered him!
Lord, give me the heart of Hezekiah,
that I will be worthy
to come to you in prayer.
Each day, I struggle to please you.
Heal me from my sins and misdeeds
when I come to you in true humility!
This is my petition, Lord,
that I will be forever in your care.
I adore you, my wonderful God!
You have given so much,
even your precious son, Jesus,
that we may learn to do your will.
I thank you, Lord,
I praise you forever!
Through Jesus Christ,
Amen!

"A man of violence entices his neighbor and leads him in a way that is not good."

—Proverbs 16:29

Violent thoughts spread like a disease,
causing suffering and sorrow.
A mind possessed by the evil one
brings pain and unhappiness
to all around them.
The evil one rejoices in this.
Only you, Lord, can heal these minds
and dispel the evil one!
Satan spreads his lies
and deceives all who are unaware of his wiles.
My Lord and my God,
make me aware at all times of Satan's evil deeds,
how he sneaks into parts of my life
when I'm preoccupied!
Protect my loved ones, in the name of Jesus!
Do not allow Satan to provoke them to violence,
to destroy the work the Holy Spirit
is doing here on earth.
I pray I will listen
when the Holy Spirit warns me
of the evil one's approach!
Through Jesus Christ,
Amen!

"Therefore let us draw near with confidence to the throne of grace, so that we may receive mercy and find grace to help in time of need."

—*Hebrews 4:16*

Grace, a gift, an unmerited gift!
While I would not often refuse a worldly gift,
I frequently ignore the unmerited gift from you!
Forgive me, Lord,
for yielding to the temptations of the world
and for turning away from the grace
you have so freely given to me.
Yet, Lord, you do not whisk it away from me
as I deserve,
but patiently wait for me to accept it.
Grace, so often unused, awaits my attention.
Your precious son died as a man to give us this gift;
I will hold this gift near to my heart.
Thank you, Lord.
Through Jesus Christ,
Amen!

"And forgive us our debts, as we also have forgiven our debtors."

—Matthew 6:12

Precious Lord, how many times
this verse has come from my lips,
and yet, the phrase
"as we also have forgiven our debtors"
never stood out before.
When we come to you and ask for forgiveness,
we must have already forgiven our debtors!
My precious Savior,
when I begin to say this prayer,
help me to remember
that I need to forgive others first.
For then I will be worthy to be forgiven.
Thank you, my Lord and God.
Through Jesus Christ,
Amen!

"I know that You can do all things, and that no purpose of Yours can be thwarted."

—Job 42:2

Lord, it is so good to know that Satan
cannot foil any purpose of yours.
Job was tested mightily.
He remained faithful to the Lord,
though he did not understand his fate.
My God, you allowed Satan to test Job
for you knew that Job would not fail you!
Lord, only you know what I can endure.
When I look to you,
you will not allow me to be tested
beyond my strength.
My power comes from you.
I pray, Lord, that I will allow the Holy Spirit
to guide me through all my trials and sufferings.
Then I will withstand
all that the evil one throws at me!
I thank you, Lord,
through Jesus Christ,
Amen!

"The Lord said to Satan, 'From where do you come?' Then Satan answered the Lord and said, 'From roaming about on the earth, and walking around on it.'"

—*Job 1:7*

My God and my protector,
keep Satan from me as he wanders the earth!
I pray that you will not let him touch me
or lead me into evil.
I need your strength to resist his charms.
May the Holy Spirit let me know when Satan is near,
that I may be sure to put up my shield!
I praise you, Lord;
you have given me the weapons
to resist the evil one.
You are mightier than he!
May I warn others about him when he is near,
so he cannot lure them
into temptation and destroy them.
Save those I love from his snares.
Through Jesus Christ,
Amen!

"... and God is faithful, who will not allow you to be tempted beyond what you are able, but with the temptation will provide the way of escape also, that you may be able to endure it."

—*I Corinthians 10:13*

O Lord, I am so grateful
that you look after me!
Satan, the evil one,
is so alluring and seductive.
He attempts to lure me in before I know it is him.
It is you, Lord, who awakens me to his
charms and gives me strength to
to resist his charisma.
Satan knows my weaknesses
and comes when my spirits are low.
But you, my God, are there to protect me,
to draw a veil between the evil one and me.
I pray, my Lord,
rescue me before I fall victim
to his temptations;
warn me when I must resist him!
Through Jesus Christ,
Amen!

"Indeed, there is not a righteous man on earth who continually does good and who never sins."

—*Ecclesiastes 7:20*

My Lord, my God!
My righteous Lord!
Lord, I want to stay on the path
you have planned for me.
There are so many temptations
from the evil one in this world.
Lord, at times I take the wrong way
and suffer pain.
My thoughts become confused.
Protect me, Lord!
Only you can withstand all of Satan's lures,
for you are all powerful!
You can protect me.
Resisting Satan will make me stronger.
I will be perfect only when I join you in Heaven.
Give me compassion for others
who stray from the path,
that I may help them be restored.
Through Jesus Christ,
the only perfect man who lived on this earth,
Amen!

"So David was afraid of the Lord that day; and he said, 'How can the ark of the Lord come to me?'"

—*II Samuel 6:9*

My Lord,
you traveled with the Israelites in an ark.
Your presence was with them day and night.
I desire to have your presence with me.
My heart will be opened to you, my God;
I will carry you gently.
I will keep my heart pure for you.
I will let others see your presence
by the joy that is within me!
It will be on my countenance!
I will make in my heart an ark for you, Lord!
When I obey your commands
I know you are within me!
You forgive me when I slip!
My heart will never forget your presence;
you are the joy in my life!
Keep me pure, Lord!
Through Jesus,
Amen!

". . . and you shall know the truth, and the truth will make you free."

—John 8:32

Precious Jesus,
the truth made me free
from all the mistakes of my past.
It set me free from the bondage of sin.
For you are the one who died for me
to save me from my misdeeds.
You died to free me from the bondage
that Satan put me under.
Thank you, Lord, for setting me free.
I praise you, my precious Lord;
I have read your Word.
In you, I am forgiven,
washed clean in your blood.
Praise to you, Jesus,
for being the sacrificial lamb!
Praise the Lord all day long!
Through Jesus Christ,
Amen!

"But seek first His kingdom and His righteousness, and all of these things will be added to you."

—Matthew 6:33

My precious Lord and Savior,
where shall I seek your kingdom?
I will seek it within my heart,
for there I desire you to reside.
In my heart, you will be above all things.
For how can I forget you
when you are a part of me?
I will seek your kingdom
and your righteousness in all I do.
I will rejoice in your loving presence.
Your light-filled presence
will guide my steps
in the way you desire me to go!
Make my heart ready for you;
forgive me, Lord, for my offenses.
Make my heart pure!
My God, my God, I praise you
above all else!
Through Jesus Christ,
Amen!

"Your word I have treasured in my heart, that I may not sin against You."

—Psalms 119:11

Your Word is always with me, Lord.
When I need faith,
I remember the mustard seed.
When I need love,
I remember Christ sacrificed himself to redeem me.
When I am lonely or need courage,
I think of the Holy Spirit by my side.
When I feel burdened,
I give my burden to Jesus.
When I am in a bad situation,
I pray for the Holy Spirit to give me words to say.
When I am ill, I pray for Jesus's healing hands.
When I am tempted,
I remember God will not allow me to be tempted
beyond what I am able to bear.
When a loved one does not walk with Jesus,
I give them over to Jesus.
When the world overwhelms me,
I think of Jesus's arms around me, keeping me safe.
All this comes from reading your Word, O Lord.
Praise the Lord!
Through Jesus Christ,
Amen!

"Splendor and majesty are before Him, strength and beauty are in His sanctuary."

—*Psalms 96:6*

My wonderful Lord, my God.
When I see the beauty you have given
your people to enjoy,
my heart fills with gratitude!
I can see you in the beauty!
Its greatness
is beyond our understanding.
The moon and the stars show the depth
and endless universe that are yours!
And like the universe,
your love and forgiveness
are too great to comprehend.
I can never earn your love,
yet your love is unending!
I praise you in the morning,
and all the day.
At night I go to sleep with you in my heart.
I adore only you,
I praise you, through your son, Jesus Christ.
Amen!

"So they sang praises with joy, and bowed down and worshipped."

—*II Chronicles 29:30*

Almighty God,
my mouth is filled with praises
for all you are!
I come to you with a grateful heart
for sending your son, Jesus Christ,
so we could be forgiven of our sins.
Your wonderful son,
my shepherd,
guides and protects me from the evil one.
In this, I find true joy and reason to praise you.
I keep my eyes on Jesus
so I will not lose my way.
Lord, I am so weak!
With you, I can avoid the pitfalls of this world.
Make me a servant of your will, Lord!
Through Jesus Christ,
Amen!

"Consider it all joy, my brethren, when you encounter various trials, knowing that the testing of your faith produces endurance."

—*James 1:2–3*

Yes, Lord, there is joy in my heart!
Thank you, O Lord, for this joy,
for it comes only from you!
Nothing in this world can give the joy
I have when I think of you and your wonders.
Precious Jesus,
you gave your life
that I may be free
from the bonds of this world,
so I may know the peace
that comes only from you.
Abide in me forever,
so even through trials
I will have joy in my heart.
Your joy is much more than being happy;
your joy gives me peace and contentment!
Praise Jesus!
Amen!

HOLY SPIRIT

We receive the Holy Spirit, the third person of the Trinity, when we accept Christ into our hearts. He is within us!

The Holy Spirit is our constant companion and helper! We can call on him at any time, in our work, in our prayers, in our decisions, and in our relationships.

Through the Holy Spirit, we can commune with Jesus and his Father. He comforts us with his presence. He understands all that we do or think. What a wonderful friend!

It is a wonderful feeling to know the Holy Spirit is in my life and to feel his presence in my heart!

The Holy Spirit lives in me, and I don't want him to be lonely! He is there to be called on and used to help us commune with God and to guide us in this world. The Holy Spirit also intercedes with the Father on our behalf! He has become a trusted supporter and a faithful comrade. I lean on him every day! I listen for God's words through the Holy Spirit and ask him to help me pray!

"For momentary, light affliction is producing for us an eternal weight of glory far beyond all comparison."
—*II Corinthians 4:17*

My wonderful Lord,
you have prepared for me a life eternal,
free from worry and pain.
All the trials on earth are temporary!
And yet, I fret over the daily distresses
and forget to rejoice in the glory
you have prepared
for all who love you.
Forgive me, Lord, for being so into myself.
I will take all these worldly issues as lessons
to learn to be more faithful to you.
Lord Jesus, you suffered so much for us,
but you never lost sight of the eternal joy
that awaited you in Heaven!
I shall honor you many times a day, Lord,
by thinking of you
and what you have planned for me.
I pray that the Holy Spirit will always be with me!
Remind me that when I am in the throes of self-pity,
to praise you, Lord, for your gift!
In the name of Jesus,
Amen!

"Teach me to do Your will, for You are my God; let Your good Spirit lead me on level ground."

—*Psalms 143:10*

Lord, I open my arms and heart to you,
that you may teach me thy will!
Lord, you desire good for me;
you are there to guide me into joy!
I praise you, my God;
only you can lead me in the right way,
whatever the circumstances.
How I long to be with you!
Show me the path that leads to eternity with you!
I know your Spirit is with me here on earth,
yet I desire to be in your full presence
and bask in the brilliance of your glory!
May your Spirit guide me
and keep me on a level ground.
Then I will not wander from your will!
My God, I praise you.
I trust you to bring me into your presence.
Through Jesus,
Amen!

"Now we have received, not the spirit of the world, but the Spirit who is from God, so that we might know the things freely given to us by God."

—*I Corinthians 2:12*

O marvelous God,
how you must care for me
to give your Holy Spirit to reside within!
For your Spirit knows your thoughts
and can deliver them to me.
But how often
have I denied
that I can hear these thoughts
and have continued to do my own will?
I pray, Lord, that looking to the Spirit within me
will become a natural part of
my day,
my thoughts,
my decisions,
my way of life.
Lord, I do yearn
for you to be in my thoughts always!
I will listen for the Spirit's words.
Through Jesus Christ,
Amen!

"Do you not know that you are a temple of God and that the Spirit of God dwells in you?"

—*I Corinthians 3:16*

Precious Jesus died
so I could receive the Holy Spirit.
The Holy Spirit is within me.
The Holy Spirit is joy.
The Holy Spirit is love.
The Holy Spirit is laughter.
The Holy Spirit is a comforter.
The Holy Spirit is an intercessor.
The Holy Spirit is a helper.
The Holy Spirit is a gift.
The Holy Spirit is peace.
The Holy Spirit is gentle.
The Holy Spirit is pure.
The Holy Spirit is mercy.
The Holy Spirit is a teacher.
The Holy Spirit is patience.
The Holy Spirit is kind.
The Holy Spirit is good.
The Holy Spirit is faithful.
Thank you, Lord!
Amen!

"Give ear and hear my voice. Listen and hear my words."

—*Isaiah 28:23*

My loving Father, you spoke directly to Isaiah,
and Isaiah spoke to his people.
You have taken time to give me ways to
communicate with you.
You have given me the Holy Spirit
to help me know you, Lord.
How selfish not to listen to you,
my Lord and my God.
How much you want to communicate with me.
Yet, time after time,
I want to do things my way, in my time.
I come to you when things go wrong!
I pray I will always come to you first,
for all my life.
Through Jesus Christ,
Amen!

". . . for the Holy Spirit will teach you in that very hour what you ought to say."

—Luke 12:12

O Father,
thank you for the Holy Spirit
to guide me in all things.
In the hour when words elude me,
I trust him to give me the words to say.
Then I know that the words will uplift you
and edify those who hear!
You alone, Lord, know what others
need to hear from you.
Let me be your voice
to encourage those who are perplexed!
When there is sorrow,
may my tongue speak words of comfort!
When there is emptiness,
give me words of hope!
When there is loneliness,
may I speak words of love!
Through Jesus Christ,
Amen!

"For You are my lamp, O Lord; and the Lord illumines my darkness."

—II Samuel 22:29

Though dark clouds surround me
and my heart is discontent,
I know you are near, my Lord, my God.
What is hiding in this darkness?
Sorrow, pain, unforgiveness?
Bring it to the light, O my God,
that I may see and know
what I must do to overcome this heaviness.
I will wait on you, my healer,
to show me the way to the light again.
I pray that the Holy Spirit within me
tells me what I must do;
then I will do it, Lord!
My wonderful Lord, you never fail me.
I will continue to praise you
until the life-giving water covers me!
Praise God!
Through Jesus Christ,
Amen!

"I delight to do Your will, O my God; Your Law is within my heart."

—Psalms 40:8

My ever-patient Lord,
though I delight in you,
I do not always do as you desire!
How easy it is to forget and do as I want,
giving in to the evil one!
Lord, I will strive all my days
to do as you want me to,
according to the laws you have set down!
I will remember to put on the armor of salvation.
I will call upon the Holy Spirit for guidance.
Only your plan for me is necessary
for my joy and fulfillment.
Each day is a challenge to face worldly lures
that want to keep me from you.
I adore you only, my God.
You alone do I worship.
Through Jesus Christ,
Amen!

"'. . . for this son of mine was dead, and has come to life again; he was lost and has been found.' And they began to celebrate."

—*Luke 15:24*

O mighty God, when I have strayed,
then returned,
you were quick to embrace me!
So many around me have never known you;
others have strayed.
Lord, help me to reach those people
to bring them your word, hope, and love!
May the Holy Spirit within me bring
the right words,
at the right time,
so that they will seek you and find you.
Lord, I pray that all who have strayed from you
will find a need in their hearts,
an emptiness,
so they will search for you.
Only through you can they be brought back.
Only through Jesus can they have salvation!
Thank you, Lord,
Amen!

"The Levites, their relatives, had charge of the treasures of the house of God, and of the treasures of the dedicated gifts."

—*I Chronicles 26:20*

I also have charge of the many gifts
you have given to me, my God.
Not treasures of gold and jewels, but of Jesus,
the Holy Spirit, and salvation!
They are worth far more than any treasure on earth,
yet I sometimes take them for granted
and do not show my gratitude
for such great gifts.
Without Jesus, we would not have the
Holy Spirit and our salvation.
Lord, I do need the Holy Spirit to guide me
in all my paths.
You have done all these things
that we may have eternal life.
I will hold these gifts in my heart
and remember them all my days.
Praise be to you, my God.
Through Jesus,
Amen!

"I will ask the Father, and He will give you another Helper, that He may be with you forever."

—John 14:16

Such a wonderful gift you sent, Lord,
when Jesus left this earth to claim his throne!
The Holy Spirit, the Comforter and Helper!
Always within me and ready to help me
through your grace.
Thank you, my God, for the Helper
who helps me through my troubles!
The Holy Spirit gives me the words to say
when life is so dire
that I cannot express myself!
The Holy Spirit guides my steps,
and when I stumble,
he helps me stand again.
Even when I do not ask,
he knows what I need.
He brings forth his words from my mouth.
Sometimes, I forget that he is within me,
and speak to him as if he is in another world.
Knowing that he is in my heart
comforts my soul.
I have peace.
Through Jesus Christ,
Amen.

"But will God indeed dwell with mankind on the earth? Behold, heaven and the highest heaven cannot contain You; how much less this house which I have built."

—*II Chronicles 6:18*

My Lord, I praise you for your greatness!
Indeed, you are too great to be contained
in any church
we can build for you!
But you, O Lord, found another way
to dwell with us on earth!
When precious Jesus offered himself
as a sacrificial lamb,
rose from the grave,
and taught his disciples,
he told them he would send a helper,
the Holy Spirit.
He came to dwell within us.
You are always here within me on earth, Lord,
to guide me in my life,
so it can be lived for you!
How can I ever doubt your love?
Through Jesus Christ,
Amen!

"In the same way the Spirit also helps our weakness, for we do not know how to pray as we should, but the Spirit Himself intercedes for Us with groanings too deep for words!"

—Romans 8:26

Holy Lord, when I kneel to pray,
words do not come!
My heart is too full of need.
Then I remember the Holy Spirit within me.
I wait for the Spirit, listen for the Spirit.
The Lord knows what is within me
and my most intimate needs,
needs that I am unaware of.
The Holy Spirit intercedes for me!
What a wonderful Lord you are
to provide me with the helper,
the Holy Spirit!
My God, you know all.
You give all that is necessary.
I praise you, my Lord.
Through Jesus Christ,
Amen!

*"For we wanted to come to You—I, Paul, more than once—
and yet Satan hindered us."*

—I Thessalonians 2:18

Almighty God,
how often has Satan put obstacles in my way
when you have a plan for me?
The evil one has thrown illness, pain,
temptation,
and work in my path,
all to keep me from concentrating on you!
Almighty God,
you are omnipresent and all-encompassing.
By focusing on you,
I will overcome.
The Holy Spirit is within me
and will bind the evil one
so I will not be distracted
from the right path.
I call on the Holy Spirit to protect me
from the fiery darts of Satan!
Through Jesus Christ,
Amen!

"Then I heard the voice of the Lord saying, 'Whom shall I send, and who will go for us?' Then I said, 'Here am I. Send me!'"

—*Isaiah 6:8*

Wherever you want me to go, O Lord!
I am eager to serve you
as you desire to be served!
I will honor you
and speak praise of you
to all I meet!
Those who need you surround me,
and yet sometimes I do not see them.
Give me sight to see all who need
your love and salvation!
May the Holy Spirit
give me the words to say
that they may learn of you.
Lord, send me!
Send me to those next door;
send me to the homes of the poor!
Send me across the land
and over the seas!
Send me.
Through Jesus Christ,
Amen!

"I will rejoice greatly in the Lord, My soul will exult in my God."

—*Isaiah 61:10*

Rejoice, rejoice,
O my soul
who knows the Lord!
For he is a righteous God
and will never forsake me!
His patience and gentleness
in guiding me is endless.
I thank you, Lord!
I will praise you every moment
through my words and actions!
There is only one God;
the God of all creation.
Mighty and faithful are you, God!
I lift my hands and shout your praise!
I praise you for sending your only son
to be a sacrifice for my sins.
I praise you for sending
the Holy Spirit,
to guide me through this world full of pitfalls.
Through Jesus Christ,
Amen!

"And when He had said this, He breathed on them and said to them, 'Receive the Holy Spirit.'"

—*John 20:22*

Lord, thank you for this body.
It was created and loved by you.
Therefore, Lord,
I will care for it as home of the Holy Spirit,
keeping it clean, taking care of it
as I would any temple of yours!
I will nourish it
with the words of the Holy Bible.
I will feed it
the wonderful food you have provided.
I will exercise
my body and mind
so I will be strong and ready to serve you.
It does not matter if my body is not perfect,
if there is pain,
if it has weaknesses
or becomes ill.
With you, Lord,
I have peace and strength to serve you!
I praise you, Lord; your works are wonderful!
Through Jesus,
Amen!

HOPE

". . . and hope does not disappoint, because the love of God has been poured out within our hearts through the Holy Spirit which was given to us" (Romans 5:5).

Without hope, we would be lost! We put our hope in people, education, vehicles, and jobs, but only hope in God will not disappoint. When all is dark, hope is that ion of light that keeps us holding on and moving forward.

Over the years, I have had many periods of depression—deep, deep darkness—and wondered if I would ever come out of it! I did climb out of the pit, not by myself, but by the grace of God! The evil one could not hold me back from what God wanted me to do. Our precious Lord is the light of hope that I have clung to over the years. Praise the Lord for giving us hope!

"He lay down and slept under a juniper tree; and behold, there was an angel touching him and he said to him, 'Arise, eat.'"

—*I Kings 19:5*

Elijah walked with God,
yet felt he had failed
and asked to die.
Food and water were brought by an angel
to sustain him!
Fearful, Elijah hid.
In the cave, Elijah listened to you, Lord,
and went forth to do your bidding.
O Lord, when I felt I have failed you,
you alone sustained me
with your unconditional love.
You are patience eternal!
You sent me forth to seek out your will for me.
I have again risen
to serve only you, my God!
Through Jesus Christ,
Amen!

"They who dwell in the ends of the earth stand in awe of Your signs; You make the dawn and the sunset shout for joy."

—*Psalms 65:8*

My amazing God,
wonderful is your name!
Each day brings a new awakening
of your creation:
a flower in an unexpected place;
an eagle spreading its wings,
softly, steadily rising above the trees;
ducklings walking across the street;
children running on the grass;
a homeless man, getting a bed for the night
by his "neighbor";
adult children visiting their parents.
I see you in all these things, Lord.
I see your love,
your creativity,
your care for each creature!
Through Jesus Christ,
Amen!

"You who have shown me many troubles and distresses, will revive me again, and will bring me up again from the depths of the earth."

—*Psalms 71:20*

How many times, my Lord,
have I worked myself into a pit of self-pity?
Then I cry to you for help!
You have given me the freedom to go my own way.
When I see what a mess I have made,
you are there,
ready to help me out of the pit of self-destruction.
These are times of learning to trust
to come to you first, O Lord.
When I ignore you and go my own way,
you allow me free will.
I am drawn by worldly things
that draw me away from you.
You have always been there to help me up!
Now I come to you and trust in you,
to avoid falling into the pit.
You guide me all the way!
Thank you, my Lord and God!
Through Jesus Christ,
Amen!

"And those who know Your name will put their trust in You: for you, O Lord, have not forsaken those who seek You."

—*Psalms 9:10*

O almighty God, you have not forsaken me!
Even when I feel alone, you are there.
I just need to reach out,
to speak to you,
and you will answer!
You sent your only son
to die for me.
Jesus did not die to leave me on my own,
but to show me how much he loves me
and to be with me forever.
I praise you, holy God!
I praise you at the rising sun!
I praise you when the sun is high
and when it sets!
I praise you when I see the moon and stars!
Everything is as you planned it.
I am where you have planned for me to be, too.
Thank you, my Lord and my God!
Through Jesus Christ,
Amen!

"In the light of a king's face is life, and his favor is like a cloud with the spring rain."

—*Proverbs 16:15*

Lord, you have made some clouds
heavy and dark that roil and turn in anger.
There are clouds like light puffs of frozen breath
against a blue, blue sky!
When my heart is heavy,
I think upon these things.
I remember that you made them all
and that you can take them away!
I know they are there for a reason.
When there are clouds in my life,
I know that there is life-giving water in them.
I pray that I will never let a dark cloud distract
me from following you!
I will look beyond and see the blessings
you have for me!
Through Jesus Christ,
Amen!

"Yet those who wait for the Lord will gain new strength."

—*Isaiah 40:31*

Lord, this I know:
you are the source of my strength
physically,
mentally,
emotionally,
spiritually.
I wait on you to renew me
whenever I am in need.
When the evil one strikes
and puts obstacles in my way,
I depend on you, my Lord.
You are my light in the darkness,
the hand that guides me!
You are the wisdom I need
to grow spiritually.
I wait on you, my Lord.
Through Jesus Christ,
Amen!

"... and hope does not disappoint, because the love of God has been poured out within our hearts through the Holy Spirit who was given to us."

—*Romans 5:5*

I have a future,
I have a hope.
You have planned it that way,
my wonderful Lord.
From the beginning
you have known
what plans you have for each of us.
There is always a glimmer of hope,
a sliver of light
when I search for you.
When I trust in your plan for me,
then I can see where to go!
I only need to know the next step,
not the years ahead.
You are always with me!
I lift my voice to praise you,
to tell others of your love!
Through Jesus Christ,
Amen!

"He makes the winds His messengers."

—*Psalms 104:4*

My Lord, my God!
What a beautiful sight out my window!
The wind gently blowing across
the fresh, pure snow,
lifting swirls of snow that ripple up the hill!
And yet, I feel my heart is empty,
yearning for something that eludes me.
What will give me fullness in my heart, my God?
As I watch the wisps of snow,
I think of angels and how they surround me,
both gentle and invisible.
The wisps of snow could be stirred by their wings!
Then I remember that you are always
near and waiting for me to communicate with you.
My wonderful Lord, my hope is in you,
always near, always constant.
Through Jesus Christ,
Amen!

"For You have rescued my soul from death, my eyes from tears, my feet from stumbling."

—*Psalms 116:8*

My God and my Savior,
indeed, you have lifted my soul
from the hands of the evil one
through the blood of Jesus!
I praise you and thank you for this
wonderful, loving act.
Many times you have dried my tears
when the sorrows of this world oppressed me.
I was too weak to overcome them by myself!
But you, Lord, lifted me up with your loving arms
and comforted me.
When I started down the wrong path,
you were there to guide me
with your shepherd's staff
into the right way.
Yes, you have kept me from stumbling!
I praise you, Lord,
for your wonderful care, comfort, and salvation!
Through Jesus Christ,
Amen!

"'For I know the plans that I have for you,' declares the Lord, 'plans for welfare and not for calamity to give you a future and a hope.'"

—Jeremiah 29:11

My God of all understanding,
when I am confused about what to do,
I can count on you
to show me
the path you want me to take.
Such a comfort to know
you are leading me and completely understand
my heart and mind!
When confusion fills my mind
and the next step is dark,
I listen for your message.
I feel your gentle guiding hands
turn me in the right direction!
My trust is in you, my Lord.
Through Jesus Christ,
Amen!

"You have turned my mourning into dancing; You have loosed my sackcloth and girded me with gladness."

—Psalms 30:11

Lord, God almighty!
I praise your wonderful words;
they always give me answers!
How often you have turned my sorrow into joy,
joy that comes only from you!
Today, Lord, I will rely on you
to take away my mourning clothes
and clothe me with your wonderful joy!
So many earthly things draw me down,
causing pain.
But you lift me up, beyond the clouds
that cover my heart.
Then I feel your full glory
through my cares.
My hope is in you, O Lord, and only you!
I give you all my worries and cares,
so I will be free to praise you continually.
Through your son, Jesus, I pray,
Amen!

". . . as sorrowful yet always rejoicing . . ."

—II Corinthians 6:10

O precious Jesus,
there are times when memories come to me
of wonderful moments with a loved one
now gone from this life.
A sorrow overcomes me.
I feel a desire to relive that time.
Lord, when I put you in that memory,
I find myself rejoicing
that you gave me the experience to recall.
When I count these times as blessings from you,
then I can rejoice!
These blessings are not gone;
they can be recalled
to remind me of how wonderful you are.
Thank you, Lord, for all your blessings.
Through Jesus Christ,
Amen!

"As the deer pants for the water brooks, so my soul pants for You, O God."

—Psalms 42:1

Marvelous Lord,
creator of all,
you supply all our needs!
As you provide the water for the deer,
you satisfy my soul with your love,
your endless, perfect love!
As the graceful deer solely depends on you
to care for it,
may I depend on you for all my thirsts!
Fill me with your love and your words
that I may carry them forth to others.
My hope is in you;
I thirst for you,
I praise you forever and ever,
for all your wondrous works!
Through your son, Jesus Christ.
Amen!

"For by Him all things were created . . . all things have been created through Him and for Him."

—Colossians 1:16

Lord God, my wonderful God!
At dawn, I smell the melting snow,
the awakening earth.
I hear the sweet song of birds,
the coarse song of a mallard.
I smile.
There is a new life after the long winter.
In my heart,
I feel a new life rising,
more aware of the world around me
as God's creation.
Lord, I praise you for awakening in me a new spirit.
I pray that this new spirit will serve you
as you desire to be served!
I will honor you
with all my heart and soul!
Your presence is worth
much more than gold or precious gems.
My Lord and my God,
you are everything!
Through Jesus,
Amen!

"Lift up your eyes on high and see who has created these stars. . . He calls them all by name."

—Isaiah 40:26

Bright lights in the evening sky,
too many to count.
Lord, you have named them all!
The stars and planets lead me to
many imaginations.
I call them the heavens;
is this where you are?
What part do they play in your plan for the universe?
Are they simply for my enjoyment?
For your enjoyment?
I look for your constellations;
you have placed every one.
They give me direction in the night.
They give me beauty
and show your greatness.
My wonderful Lord and God,
you reign over all!
Amen!

"Why are you in despair, O my soul? And why have you become disturbed within me?"

—*Psalms 42:11*

My heart is broken within me, Lord,
as I think of a loved one that is far from me.
Yet I know, O Lord,
you care very much for the one I love.
My pain can only be a tiny part
of what you must have felt
as you allowed your son
to take our sins upon himself
and die on the cross to save us!
I will release the pain of my heart's sorrow.
I shall let you bless the one I love.
You will care for my loved one
better than I ever could.
Help me, Lord, to totally trust you.
I am helpless to do more.
In my weakness, you can do your wonderful works!
Through Jesus Christ,
Amen!

"Listen, my beloved brethren: did not God choose the poor of this world to be rich in faith and heirs of the kingdom which He promised to those who love Him?"

—James 2:5

Precious Jesus, you spoke of the poor so often.
You loved them and gave them hope.
I have been impoverished
in spirit,
in money,
in faith,
in hope,
in health,
in love,
in friends,
in laughter,
and in family.
In any way that I am poor, you love me
and give me hope!
Lord, give me the grace
to know those who are impoverished in any way.
Help me to encourage them,
to show them your love,
to be their friend.
I praise you, Lord, for all your goodness and love!
Through Jesus Christ,
Amen!

"Peter got out of the boat, and walked on the water and came toward Jesus."

—*Matthew 14:29*

My Lord,
you walked on the water of the sea.
Then you allowed Peter to walk on the water.
Peter had doubt and began to sink!
Lord, I do not ask to walk on the sea,
but like Peter, I have doubts.
You have given me "living water,"
which enables me to do many things
in your Holy Name.
I pray, my Lord,
that I will keep my faith in your living water!
If I should start to sink,
I trust you will take my hand
as you took Peter's
and raise me up again!
In Jesus's name,
Amen!

ACKNOWLEDGMENTS

Feather on the Water began with some prayers I wrote for dear family members and friends who were in challenging seasons of life. At the urging of many, I have collected these prayers so I may share them with a larger audience. I thank the many friends that have encouraged me. My team at Wise Ink, Amy and Laura, thank you for guiding me through this exciting process! My editor, Heidi Sheard, thanks for your great attention to detail. My designer, Kris Vetter, thank you for displaying my written prayers in such a breathtaking way! It was such a pleasure to work with a team of professionals who understood my vision for *Feather on the Water*! Above all, I praise the Lord for giving me the prayers to write!